On the Day I Died

Written by Sandra Callis

Illustrated by Christine Waugh-Fleischmann

Dedicated to
all of those who have
come before,
all of those who have
yet to be born,
and those special souls
who are with us now.

"There are more things
in heaven and earth ...
Than are dreamt of in
your philosophy."

William Shakespeare
- Hamlet (1.5.167-8),
Hamlet to Horatio

On the day I died,
I looked toward the foot of my bed
and saw my mommy and daddy,
young and excited,
just like the day I was born!

On the day I died,
we went to the beach and
danced in the sand,
the water licking at our toes.

On the day I died,
we were dancing and
twirling, and
I saw all of my grandmothers
and grandfathers
walking toward us
from the horizons.
They were filled with joy
and joined our dance.
I heard them say,
"We are so proud of you."

On the day I died,
my family parted along the beach, and
the earth thundered under
the paws and hooves
of the spirit animals I love.
The waves crashed as
sea animals breached.
The skies churned with the
flurry of my winged allies.

On the day I died,
the heavens opened up,
and I gasped at the
sight of my spirit guides.
I saw my healing ancestors,
my guardian angels,
all of my teachers from the
East, South, West and North,
from Below and Above,
from the Past and the Future.

Our dance slowed.

On the day I died,
our dance swirled and swayed,
until we all joined into the misty fog
and rose slowly into space.

On the day I died,
we twirled in space for
a thousand, maybe
a million years.
Longer than you
can imagine.

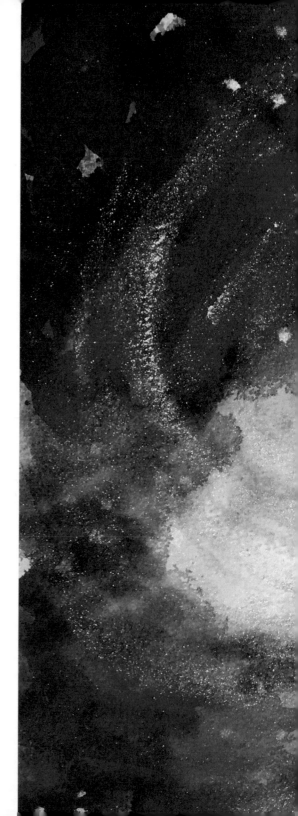

On the day I died,
I and everything I love
were drawn along beams
toward the sun.

On the day I died,
the sun lapped us up,
and we danced up and down,
round and round,
screaming for joy.
The music made us
giggle and jump.
I never laughed so
hard as I did
while I danced on the sun
for a thousand, maybe
a million, years.

On the day I died,
we danced and danced.

On the day I died,
thousands of souls
joined the dance,
until the surface of the sun
got heavier and heavier,
and we were drawn in
toward the dark center.

I was afraid, but I was not alone.

On the day I died,
the sun caved in and then spit me
and all of my spirits
into space on a huge rock.
Space was dark.
We flew past planets, asteroids,
and other suns.
We were quiet, but we were not alone.
We travelled for thousands,
maybe millions, of years.

On the day I died,
we grew bored with simply flying along.
The spirit of bear started to cover
himself with dirt and water,
and we were so excited to
see his mud costume.
We all did the same thing.
Soon we were moving around and
enjoying each other's new body.
Now we could see everybody clearly,
and we could touch each other.

On the day I died,
all of my beloved spirits
came back to life on Earth.

On the day I died,
I found that keeping a body
together was hard work.
Mud will cake and dry.
I had to continue to draw
from the Earth and
get help from other spirits.
Sometimes spirits would lose their bodies.
I was sad I couldn't see
them or touch them,
but I knew they were still around.

On the day I died,
my body died again and again,
but I kept making new
ones from the Earth.
Each looked different,
but it was still me.
I worked very hard
for thousands, maybe
millions, of years.

On the day I died,
I grew tired.
I asked all the other spirits,
"Why do we keep doing this?
Why don't we dance in the fog
or find another sun?"

And the Great Spirit whispered in my ear,
"Look around you."

So I did.

On the day I died,
I saw:
A baby's little fingers, with
their tiny fingernails.
A cascading waterfall, its
spray like white lace.
A slow brook running
over rounded stones.
Emerald hillsides, and
oh, so much more.
I saw how beautiful the spirits
had made everything.

On the day I died,
I rested.
I felt myself go to sleep,
except I could still think.
My spirit shrunk and shrunk,
until it became a little white
seed, glistening like an opal.

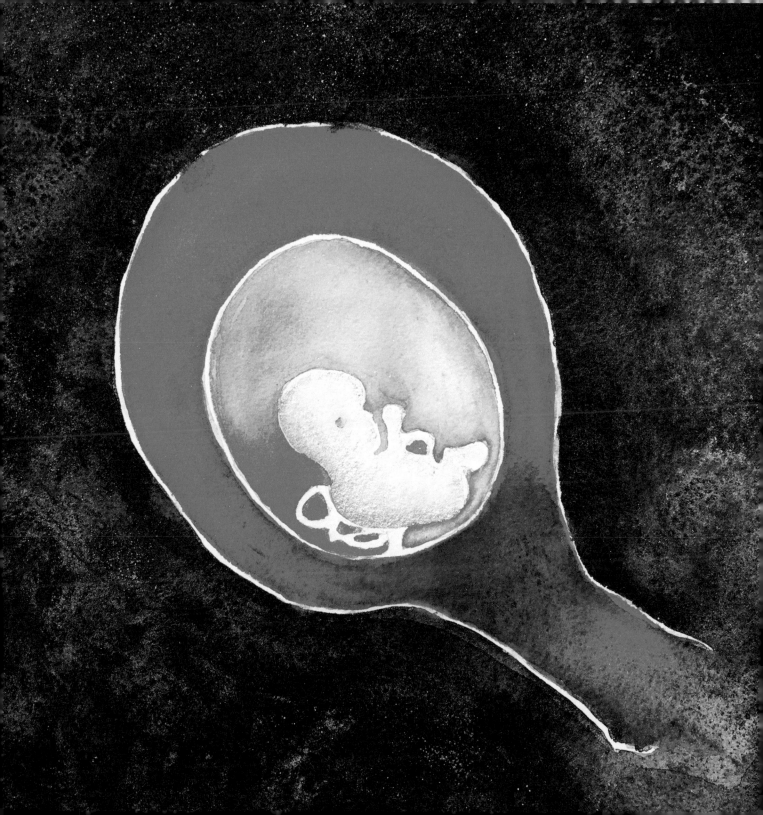

On the day I died,
I learned my own nature.

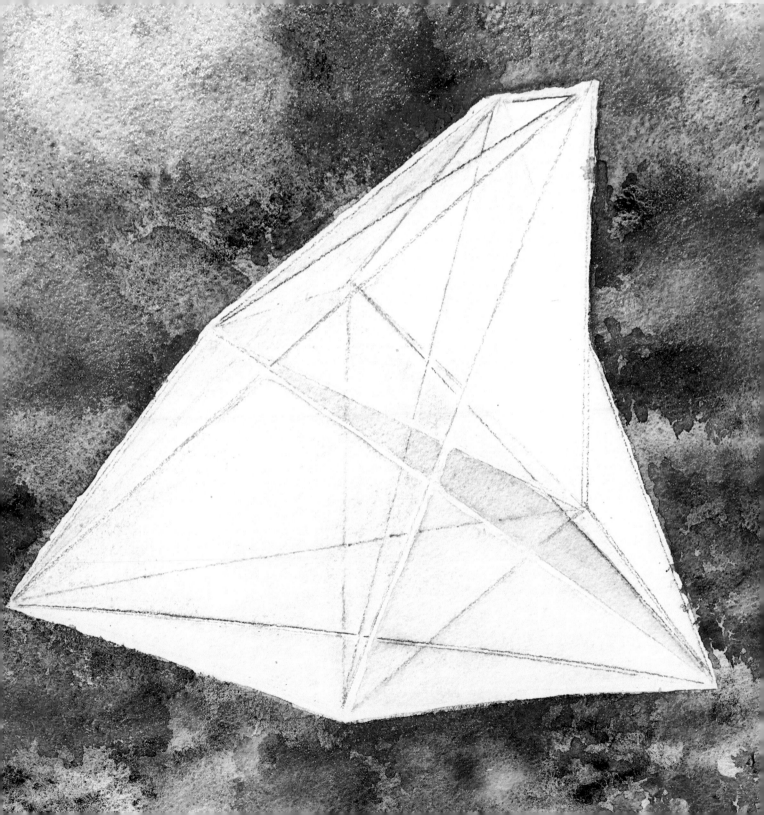

On the day I died,
I learned:
My ancestors are as excited
on the day I die as on
the day I was born.
The animals I love and spirit
guides are with me forever.
Everything grows, shrinks,
changes, and endures.
Life on Earth is very hard,
but the Earth is beautiful.
Singing and dancing makes
everything happy.
I am never alone or gone.

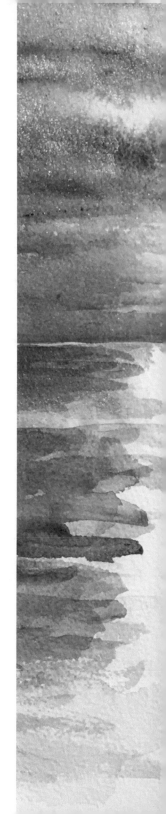

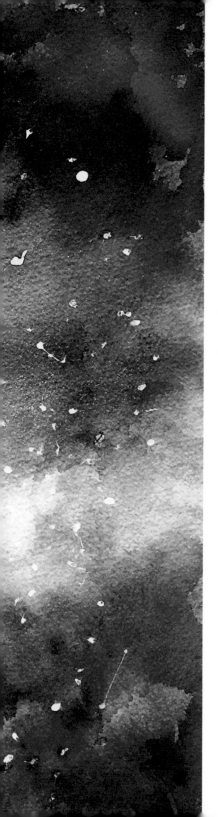

On the day I died,
I learned that
I am a creative seed
that grows and enriches
the planets, the air, the moon,
the sun, the stars, deep space,
and all of creation.

We will meet again, and
you will know me.

Balboa Press books may be ordered through booksellers or by contacting:

Balboa Press
A Division of Hay House
1663 Liberty Drive
Bloomington, IN 47403
www.balboapress.com
1 (877) 407-4847

ISBN: 978-1-9822-1844-7 (sc)
ISBN: 978-1-9822-1843-0 (e)

Library of Congress Control Number: 2018914823

Print information available on the last page.

Balboa Press rev. date: 12/18/2018

BALBOA.
PRESS
A DIVISION OF HAY HOUSE

Printed in the United States
By Bookmasters